MAD LIBS®

PIRATES MAD LIBS

By Roger Price and Leonard Stern

PRICE STERN SLOAN

PRICE STERN SLOAN
Published by the Penguin Group
Penguin Group (USA) Inc., 375 Hudson Street, New York, New York 10014, USA
Penguin Group (Canada), 90 Eglinton Avenue East, Suite 700,
Toronto, Ontario, Canada M4P 2Y3
(a division of Pearson Penguin Canada Inc.)
Penguin Books Ltd, 80 Strand, London WC2R 0RL, England
Penguin Ireland, 25 St Stephen's Green, Dublin 2, Ireland (a division of Penguin Books Ltd)
Penguin Group (Australia), 250 Camberwell Road, Camberwell, Victoria 3124, Australia
(a division of Pearson Australia Group Pty Ltd)
Penguin Books India Pvt Ltd, 11 Community Centre,
Panchsheel Park, New Delhi-110 017, India
Penguin Group (NZ), 67 Apollo Drive, Mairangi Bay, Auckland 1311, New Zealand
(a division of Pearson New Zealand Ltd)
Penguin Books (South Africa) (Pty) Ltd, 24 Sturdee Avenue,
Rosebank, Johannesburg 2196, South Africa

Penguin Books Ltd, Registered Offices:
80 Strand, London WC2R 0RL, England

Copyright © 2007 by Price Stern Sloan.
All rights reserved.

Published by Price Stern Sloan,
a division of Penguin Young Readers Group,
345 Hudson Street, New York, New York 10014.

Printed in the United States of America. No part of this publication may be reproduced,
stored in any retrieval system, or transmitted, in any form or by any means, electronic,
mechanical, photocopying, or otherwise, without the prior written permission of the publisher.

ISBN 978-0-8431-2313-5

15 17 19 20 18 16

PSS! and *MAD LIBS* are registered trademarks of Penguin Group (USA) Inc.

MAD LIBS
INSTRUCTIONS

MAD LIBS® is a game for people who don't like games!
It can be played by one, two, three, four, or forty.

• RIDICULOUSLY SIMPLE DIRECTIONS

In this tablet you will find stories containing blank spaces where words
are left out. One player, the READER, selects one of these stories. The
READER does not tell anyone what the story is about. Instead, he/she asks
the other players, the WRITERS, to give him/her words. These words are
used to fill in the blank spaces in the story.

• TO PLAY

The READER asks each WRITER in turn to call out a word—an adjective or
a noun or whatever the space calls for—and uses them to fill in the blank
spaces in the story. The result is a MAD LIBS® game.

When the READER then reads the completed MAD LIBS® game to the other
players, they will discover that they have written a story that is fantastic,
screamingly funny, shocking, silly, crazy, or just plain dumb—depending
upon which words each WRITER called out.

• EXAMPLE (*Before* and *After*)

"_____ !" he said _____
      EXCLAMATION   ADVERB

as he jumped into his convertible _____ and
                                NOUN

drove off with his _____ wife.
                 ADJECTIVE

"*Ouch!* !" he said *Stupidly*
      EXCLAMATION   ADVERB

as he jumped into his convertible *cat* and
                           NOUN

drove off with his *brave* wife.
               ADJECTIVE

MAD LIBS
QUICK REVIEW

In case you have forgotten what adjectives, adverbs, nouns, and verbs are, here is a quick review:

An ADJECTIVE describes something or somebody. Lumpy, soft, ugly, messy, and short are adjectives.

An ADVERB tells how something is done. It modifies a verb and usually ends in "ly." Modestly, stupidly, greedily, and carefully are adverbs.

A NOUN is the name of a person, place, or thing. Sidewalk, umbrella, bridle, bathtub, and nose are nouns.

A VERB is an action word. Run, pitch, jump, and swim are verbs. Put the verbs in past tense if the directions say PAST TENSE. Ran, pitched, jumped, and swam are verbs in the past tense.

When we ask for A PLACE, we mean any sort of place: a country or city (Spain, Cleveland) or a room (bathroom, kitchen).

An EXCLAMATION or SILLY WORD is any sort of funny sound, gasp, grunt, or outcry, like Wow!, Ouch!, Whomp!, Ick!, and Gadzooks!

When we ask for specific words, like a NUMBER, a COLOR, an ANIMAL, or a PART OF THE BODY, we mean a word that is one of those things, like seven, blue, horse, or head.

When we ask for a PLURAL, it means more than one. For example, cat pluralized is cats.

MAD LIBS® is fun to play with friends, but you can also play it by yourself! To begin with, DO NOT look at the story on the page below. Fill in the blanks on this page with the words called for. Then, using the words you have selected, fill in the blank spaces in the story.

Now you've created your own hilarious MAD LIBS® game!

TALK LIKE A PIRATE

NOUN _____

ADJECTIVE _____

VERB _____

ADVERB _____

NOUN _____

ADJECTIVE _____

PLURAL NOUN _____

PLURAL NOUN _____

PLURAL NOUN _____

PART OF THE BODY _____

NOUN _____

NOUN _____

NOUN _____

NOUN _____

PART OF THE BODY _____

MAD LIBS

TALK LIKE A PIRATE

Ye can always pretend to be a bloodthirsty _____,

NOUN

threatening everyone by waving yer _____ sword

ADJECTIVE

in the air, but until ye learn to _____ like a pirate,

VERB

ye'll never be _____ accepted as an authentic

ADVERB

_____. So here's what ye do: Cleverly work into yer

NOUN

daily conversations _____ pirate phrases such as

ADJECTIVE

"Ahoy there, _____," "Avast, ye _____,"

PLURAL NOUN   PLURAL NOUN

and "Shiver me _____." Remember to drop all yer *gs*

PLURAL NOUN

when ye say such words as *sailin'*, *spittin'*, and *fightin'*. This will

give ye a/an _____ start to being recognized as a

PART OF THE BODY

swashbucklin' _____. Once ye have the lingo down

NOUN

pat, it helps to wear a three-cornered _____ on yer

NOUN

head, stash a/an _____ in yer pants, and keep a/an

NOUN

_____ perched atop yer _____. Aye,

NOUN   PART OF THE BODY

now ye be a real pirate!

From PIRATES MAD LIBS® • Copyright © 2007 by Price Stern Sloan, a division of
Penguin Young Readers Group, 345 Hudson Street, New York, NY 10014.

MAD LIBS® is fun to play with friends, but you can also play it by yourself! To begin with, DO NOT look at the story on the page below. Fill in the blanks on this page with the words called for. Then, using the words you have selected, fill in the blank spaces in the story.

Now you've created your own hilarious MAD LIBS® game!

JOLLY ROGER

NOUN _____

NOUN _____

ADJECTIVE _____

PLURAL NOUN _____

ADJECTIVE _____

PLURAL NOUN _____

PLURAL NOUN _____

NOUN _____

PLURAL NOUN _____

NOUN _____

PART OF THE BODY _____

PART OF THE BODY _____

NOUN _____

ADJECTIVE _____

PLURAL NOUN _____

ADJECTIVE _____

NOUN _____

PLURAL NOUN _____

MAD LIBS

JOLLY ROGER

The black-and-white _____ that waved in the breeze
                              NOUN

atop a pirate ship was called a Jolly Roger. There are many theories

as to how the Jolly _____ got its _____
                          NOUN   ADJECTIVE

name, but most _____ agree that the _____
                      PLURAL NOUN   ADJECTIVE

flag was designed to scare the living _____ out of
                                            PLURAL NOUN

captains and crews on merchant _____. And indeed, it
                                      PLURAL NOUN

did. When a lookout shouted, "_____ ahoy!" and the
                                      NOUN

captain sighted the dreaded skull and cross-_____
                                                  PLURAL NOUN

through his/her spy-_____, not only did it strike terror
                          NOUN

in his/her _____, but it sent chills up and down the
              PART OF THE BODY

_____ of every member on the _____.
PART OF THE BODY   NOUN

However, nothing generated as much _____
                                          ADJECTIVE

fear on merchant _____ as the hoisting of a/an
                      PLURAL NOUN

_____ red flag on a pirate _____. The
ADJECTIVE   NOUN

red flag signaled that mercy would neither be asked for nor given—

no _____ would be spared.
      PLURAL NOUN

From PIRATES MAD LIBS® • Copyright © 2007 by Price Stern Sloan, a division of
Penguin Young Readers Group, 345 Hudson Street, New York, NY 10014.

MAD LIBS® is fun to play with friends, but you can also play it by yourself! To begin with, DO NOT look at the story on the page below. Fill in the blanks on this page with the words called for. Then, using the words you have selected, fill in the blank spaces in the story.

Now you've created your own hilarious MAD LIBS® game!

PIRATE MOVIES

PLURAL NOUN _____

PLURAL NOUN _____

NOUN _____

PLURAL NOUN _____

PLURAL NOUN _____

NOUN _____

PLURAL NOUN _____

NOUN _____

PLURAL NOUN _____

ADJECTIVE _____

NOUN _____

NOUN _____

PLURAL NOUN _____

ADJECTIVE _____

PLURAL NOUN _____

CELEBRITY (MALE) _____

ADJECTIVE _____

PERSON IN ROOM _____

PART OF THE BODY _____

ADJECTIVE _____

NOUN _____

MAD LIBS

PIRATE MOVIES

Even in the days of silent _____, pirate movies were
                          PLURAL NOUN

smash _____ at the box _____, earning millions
       PLURAL NOUN   NOUN

of _____. They enchanted kids and _____
    PLURAL NOUN   PLURAL NOUN

alike. But in real life, pirates were as different from the ones on

film as night and _____. They were ruthless and
                        NOUN

cold-blooded _____ who had no respect for law and
              PLURAL NOUN

_____. Movies made pirates seem as lovable as teddy
   NOUN

_____. In the 1920s in the _____ silent
 PLURAL NOUN   ADJECTIVE

film "_____," Douglas Fairbanks played the first
        NOUN

swashbuckling _____ to ever roam the seven
                    NOUN

_____ in search of _____ adventures and
 PLURAL NOUN   ADJECTIVE

_____ in distress. Today, _____ carries
 PLURAL NOUN   CELEBRITY (MALE)

on this _____ tradition with his portrayal of
           ADJECTIVE

_____ Sparrow, a tongue in-_____ pirate
 PERSON IN ROOM   PART OF THE BODY

buccaneer. Throughout the years, pirates have had a/an

_____ way of lighting up the silver _____!
   ADJECTIVE   NOUN

From PIRATES MAD LIBS® • Copyright © 2007 by Price Stern Sloan, a division of
Penguin Young Readers Group, 345 Hudson Street, New York, NY 10014.

MAD LIBS® is fun to play with friends, but you can also play it by yourself! To begin with, DO NOT look at the story on the page below. Fill in the blanks on this page with the words called for. Then, using the words you have selected, fill in the blank spaces in the story.

Now you've created your own hilarious MAD LIBS® game!

PIRATE LOYALTY OATH
(ARTICLES OF AGREEMENT)

COLOR _____

NOUN _____

PART OF THE BODY _____

TYPE OF LIQUID _____

PART OF THE BODY _____

ADJECTIVE _____

NOUN _____

PLURAL NOUN _____

NUMBER _____

PLURAL NOUN _____

NOUN _____

PLURAL NOUN _____

PART OF THE BODY _____

NOUN _____

ADJECTIVE _____

NOUN _____

NOUN _____

ADJECTIVE _____

VERB _____

NOUN _____

PLURAL NOUN _____

MAD LIBS

PIRATE LOYALTY OATH
(ARTICLES OF AGREEMENT)

Many a boy and girl dream of sailing the ocean _____
COLOR

aboard a/an _____ ship. But that dream becomes
NOUN

a nightmare when they learn that they have to prick their

_____ and sign an oath of loyalty with their own
PART OF THE BODY

_____ before they can set _____
TYPE OF LIQUID   PART OF THE BODY

aboard the ship. This is how one _____ oath might
ADJECTIVE

have read: "Any buccaneer who disobeys the captain's orders will

be put under lock and _____ and fed only bread and
NOUN

_____ for _____ days and _____.
PLURAL NOUN   NUMBER   PLURAL NOUN

Any shipmate caught trying to jump _____ will receive
NOUN

forty _____ on his or her _____. Any crew
PLURAL NOUN   PART OF THE BODY

member who strikes a fellow crew _____ shall be tied
NOUN

to a/an _____ sail from sunup to _____-down.
ADJECTIVE   NOUN

Any _____ who does not keep his or her sword
NOUN

_____ and musket ready to _____ will be
ADJECTIVE   VERB

thrown over the _____ and fed to the _____."
NOUN   PLURAL NOUN

From PIRATES MAD LIBS® • Copyright © 2007 by Price Stern Sloan, a division of
Penguin Young Readers Group, 345 Hudson Street, New York, NY 10014.

MAD LIBS® is fun to play with friends, but you can also play it by yourself! To begin with, DO NOT look at the story on the page below. Fill in the blanks on this page with the words called for. Then, using the words you have selected, fill in the blank spaces in the story.

Now you've created your own hilarious MAD LIBS® game!

PIRATE CHAIN OF COMMAND

PLURAL NOUN _____

NOUN _____

PART OF THE BODY _____

PART OF THE BODY _____

PLURAL NOUN _____

ADJECTIVE _____

PLURAL NOUN _____

NOUN _____

ADJECTIVE _____

PLURAL NOUN _____

PLURAL NOUN _____

ADJECTIVE _____

PLURAL NOUN _____

ADJECTIVE _____

ADJECTIVE _____

PLURAL NOUN _____

PLURAL NOUN _____

NOUN _____

VERB (PAST TENSE) _____

NOUN _____

NOUN _____

MAD LIBS

PIRATE CHAIN OF COMMAND

What kinds of jobs did _____ have on a pirate ship? First
                              PLURAL NOUN

there was the captain. His or her _____ was law. He or
                                          NOUN

she ruled with an iron _____. The first mate was the
                          PART OF THE BODY

captain's right-_____ man. He or she doled out everything
                  PART OF THE BODY

from _____ to punishments, and was also in charge
        PLURAL NOUN

of dividing up the _____ booty stolen from merchant
                        ADJECTIVE

_____. The boatswain was a junior _____
  PLURAL NOUN   NOUN

whose _____ tasks included hoisting the _____,
          ADJECTIVE   PLURAL NOUN

rigging the _____, and keeping the decks _____
              PLURAL NOUN   ADJECTIVE

and clear of _____. The carpenter kept the ship in tip-top,
                PLURAL NOUN

_____ shape. Without his or her _____ skills
  ADJECTIVE   ADJECTIVE

in repairing _____ and fixing damaged _____,
                PLURAL NOUN   PLURAL NOUN

a ship would have ended up in Davy Jones's _____. If you
                                              NOUN

had _____ on a pirate ship, what job would you have
      VERB (PAST TENSE)

had? The _____ of the ship? Interesting choice. You must
            NOUN

be a fearless _____.
                  NOUN

From PIRATES MAD LIBS® • Copyright © 2007 by Price Stern Sloan, a division of
Penguin Young Readers Group, 345 Hudson Street, New York, NY 10014.

MAD LIBS® is fun to play with friends, but you can also play it by yourself! To begin with, DO NOT look at the story on the page below. Fill in the blanks on this page with the words called for. Then, using the words you have selected, fill in the blank spaces in the story.

Now you've created your own hilarious MAD LIBS® game!

PIRATE PROFILE:
BARTHOLOMEW ROBERTS
(AKA BLACK BART)

ADJECTIVE _____

NOUN _____

NOUN _____

PERSON IN ROOM _____

ADJECTIVE _____

ADJECTIVE _____

NOUN _____

NOUN _____

ADJECTIVE _____

NOUN _____

NOUN _____

ADJECTIVE _____

ADJECTIVE _____

PART OF THE BODY _____

ADJECTIVE _____

PLURAL NOUN _____

PLURAL NOUN _____

PLURAL NOUN _____

NOUN _____

MAD LIBS

PIRATE PROFILE:
BARTHOLOMEW ROBERTS (AKA BLACK BART)

A/An _____ scholar once said, "You can't judge a/an
         ADJECTIVE

_____ by its _____." According to
   NOUN   NOUN

pirate historian _____, Black Bart, a ruthless and
                  PERSON IN ROOM

_____ pirate, was a/an _____ example of
   ADJECTIVE   ADJECTIVE

how looks can be deceiving. Although he was the _____
                                    NOUN

of a pirate ship, he dressed as if he were a/an _____ on
                                    NOUN

the pages of a fashion magazine. He never went into battle without

a/an _____ plume in his _____, a long-sleeved
    ADJECTIVE   NOUN

ruffled _____ tucked into his _____ breeches,
     NOUN   ADJECTIVE

and a/an _____ pearl in his left _____.
      ADJECTIVE   PART OF THE BODY

Yet in a/an _____ career that spanned a mere two
         ADJECTIVE

years and six _____, he captured more than four hundred
        PLURAL NOUN

sailing _____ and ended up with more than three
      PLURAL NOUN

hundred million _____ worth of _____.
       PLURAL NOUN   NOUN

From PIRATES MAD LIBS® • Copyright © 2007 by Price Stern Sloan, a division of
Penguin Young Readers Group, 345 Hudson Street, New York, NY 10014.

MAD LIBS® is fun to play with friends, but you can also play it by yourself! To begin with, DO NOT look at the story on the page below. Fill in the blanks on this page with the words called for. Then, using the words you have selected, fill in the blank spaces in the story.

Now you've created your own hilarious MAD LIBS® game!

BLACKBEARD INTERVIEW, PART 1

ADJECTIVE _____

ADJECTIVE _____

PERSON IN ROOM (FEMALE) _____

PERSON IN ROOM (MALE) _____

ADJECTIVE _____

VERB ENDING IN "ING" _____

NOUN _____

PLURAL NOUN _____

NOUN _____

PART OF THE BODY _____

PLURAL NOUN _____

PLURAL NOUN _____

PART OF THE BODY _____

PLURAL NOUN _____

NOUN _____

VERB ENDING IN "ING" _____

PLURAL NOUN _____

NOUN _____

ADJECTIVE _____

MAD LIBS
BLACKBEARD INTERVIEW, PART 1

This _____ interview with the _____
     ADJECTIVE   ADJECTIVE

pirate Blackbeard first appeared in *The Charleston Journal* on

April 17, 1718. It is to be performed by _____ as
                                          PERSON IN ROOM (FEMALE)

the interviewer and _____ as the interviewee.
                     PERSON IN ROOM (MALE)

Q: Have you had your _____ beard all your life?
                           ADJECTIVE

A: Arrrgh, no! I tried _____ one when I was a young
                       VERB ENDING IN "ING"

_____, but it wasn't until many _____ later
       NOUN   PLURAL NOUN

that I had a fully grown _____ on me _____.
                               NOUN   PART OF THE BODY

Q: You fly under a different flag than most _____. Why?
                                              PLURAL NOUN

A: It's me thinkin' that the skull and _____ no longer
                                         PLURAL NOUN

strikes terror into the _____ of enemy _____.
                        PART OF THE BODY   PLURAL NOUN

But when they see the flag with the skeleton and _____
                                                        NOUN

on it, they know it's Blackbeard _____ at them
                                   VERB ENDING IN "ING"

and they start quakin' in their _____. It's me calling
                                    PLURAL NOUN

_____ on the _____ seas.
       NOUN   ADJECTIVE

From PIRATES MAD LIBS® • Copyright © 2007 by Price Stern Sloan, a division of
Penguin Young Readers Group, 345 Hudson Street, New York, NY 10014.

MAD LIBS® is fun to play with friends, but you can also play it by yourself! To begin with, DO NOT look at the story on the page below. Fill in the blanks on this page with the words called for. Then, using the words you have selected, fill in the blank spaces in the story.

Now you've created your own hilarious MAD LIBS® game!

BLACKBEARD INTERVIEW, PART 2

PART OF THE BODY _____

NOUN _____

VERB _____

ADJECTIVE _____

VERB ENDING IN "ING" _____

PART OF THE BODY _____

NOUN _____

ADJECTIVE _____

NOUN _____

NOUN _____

ADJECTIVE _____

VERB ENDING IN "ING" _____

NOUN _____

ADJECTIVE _____

VERB ENDING IN "ING" _____

MAD LIBS
BLACKBEARD INTERVIEW, PART 2

Q: I hope you take no offense, sir, but it's been said that you have

a chip on your _____, you're quick to fly off the
            PART OF THE BODY

_____, and you act before you _____.
      NOUN   VERB

A: Pray to the _____ heavens that none of that be
                  ADJECTIVE

true. If it were, right now ye'd be _____with a noose
                                VERB ENDING IN "ING"

around yer _____ as sure as my name is Black-
            PART OF THE BODY

_____!
      NOUN

Q: Captain, is it true that you have more than one hundred

_____ sea chests filled with pieces of _____
      ADJECTIVE   NOUN

buried on a tropical _____?
                        NOUN

A: Blimey, ye do court danger with every _____
                                            ADJECTIVE

question. I don't like ye _____ around me monetary
                        VERB ENDING IN "ING"

affairs. Methinks it best ye take that last _____
                                                NOUN

back. A nod will do—good. Now this interview can end on a/an

_____ note and leave ye alive and _____.
      ADJECTIVE   VERB ENDING IN "ING"

Now off with ye!

From PIRATES MAD LIBS® • Copyright © 2007 by Price Stern Sloan, a division of
Penguin Young Readers Group, 345 Hudson Street, New York, NY 10014.

MAD LIBS® is fun to play with friends, but you can also play it by yourself! To begin with, DO NOT look at the story on the page below. Fill in the blanks on this page with the words called for. Then, using the words you have selected, fill in the blank spaces in the story.

Now you've created your own hilarious MAD LIBS® game!

TREASURE ISLAND

NOUN _____

NOUN _____

ADJECTIVE _____

NOUN _____

ADJECTIVE _____

PLURAL NOUN _____

NOUN _____

NUMBER _____

ADJECTIVE _____

ADJECTIVE _____

NOUN _____

ADJECTIVE _____

PART OF THE BODY _____

PART OF THE BODY _____

NOUN _____

NOUN _____

NOUN _____

ADJECTIVE _____

ADJECTIVE _____

MAD LIBS

TREASURE ISLAND

The first _____ I ever checked out of the public

NOUN

_____ was *Treasure Island* by Robert Louis Stevenson.

NOUN

I loved that _____ book so much that my dad bought

ADJECTIVE

me my own personal _____. The _____

NOUN ADJECTIVE

characters jumped right off the _____. Even today, if you

PLURAL NOUN

ask the average _____ on the street to describe a pirate,

NOUN

nine times out of _____ the answer will be, "He is a

NUMBER

broad-shouldered, _____ man with _____ hair

ADJECTIVE ADJECTIVE

on his _____, a/an _____ patch over his

NOUN ADJECTIVE

_____, a parrot on his _____, and a wooden

PART OF THE BODY PART OF THE BODY

_____ for a leg." That, almost word for _____,

NOUN NOUN

is how Stevenson described Long John Silver in *Treasure*

_____. Isn't it _____ that books can inspire so

NOUN ADJECTIVE

many generations of _____ imaginations?

ADJECTIVE

From PIRATES MAD LIBS® • Copyright © 2007 by Price Stern Sloan, a division of
Penguin Young Readers Group, 345 Hudson Street, New York, NY 10014.

MAD LIBS® is fun to play with friends, but you can also play it by yourself! To begin with, DO NOT look at the story on the page below. Fill in the blanks on this page with the words called for. Then, using the words you have selected, fill in the blank spaces in the story.

Now you've created your own hilarious MAD LIBS® game!

HOW TO THROW A PIRATE PARTY

ADJECTIVE _____

NOUN _____

NOUN _____

PLURAL NOUN _____

ADJECTIVE _____

PLURAL NOUN _____

PLURAL NOUN _____

ADJECTIVE _____

NOUN _____

ADJECTIVE _____

PART OF THE BODY _____

PART OF THE BODY (PLURAL) _____

NOUN _____

PERSON IN ROOM _____

NOUN _____

ADJECTIVE _____

MAD LIBS
HOW TO THROW
A PIRATE PARTY

If you are looking for a/an _____ way to celebrate your
ADJECTIVE

next birthday, how about a pirate-themed costume party? Start by

sending invitations in the form of a buried _____ map
NOUN

with an X marking the location of your _____. Make a
NOUN

sign for the front door that reads: "Ahoy, _____," and
PLURAL NOUN

fill the house with lots of _____ booty—Mom's silk
ADJECTIVE

_____, satin _____, and _____
PLURAL NOUN   PLURAL NOUN   ADJECTIVE

costume jewelry for starters. As your guests come aboard, tie a

bandanna around their _____, place a/an _____
NOUN   ADJECTIVE

patch over their _____, and give them fake tattoos
PART OF THE BODY

for their arms and _____. And remember,
PART OF THE BODY (PLURAL)

when the cake is presented, sing a rousing version of "Happy

Birthday" using your pirate name, like "Happy birthday, dear

_____-face _____!" Then, and only
NOUN   PERSON IN ROOM

then, may you cut the chocolate _____ with your
NOUN

_____ sword.
ADJECTIVE

From PIRATES MAD LIBS® • Copyright © 2007 by Price Stern Sloan, a division of
Penguin Young Readers Group, 345 Hudson Street, New York, NY 10014.

MAD LIBS® is fun to play with friends, but you can also play it by yourself! To begin with, DO NOT look at the story on the page below. Fill in the blanks on this page with the words called for. Then, using the words you have selected, fill in the blank spaces in the story.

Now you've created your own hilarious MAD LIBS® game!

PIRATE WEAPONS

NOUN _____

PART OF THE BODY _____

ADJECTIVE _____

PLURAL NOUN _____

PLURAL NOUN _____

ADJECTIVE _____

VERB _____

ADJECTIVE _____

PART OF THE BODY _____

NOUN _____

PLURAL NOUN _____

PLURAL NOUN _____

ADVERB _____

PART OF THE BODY _____

VERB _____

PART OF THE BODY (PLURAL) _____

ADJECTIVE _____

NOUN _____

NUMBER _____

Before attacking an enemy _____, pirates armed
_{NOUN}

themselves from head to _____ with a/an
_{PART OF THE BODY}

_____ arsenal of _____. Their three
_{ADJECTIVE} _{PLURAL NOUN}

favorite _____ were:
_{PLURAL NOUN}

1) The cutlass. Lightweight, _____-bladed, and easy
_{ADJECTIVE}

to _____—it was used in _____ quarters,
_{VERB} _{ADJECTIVE}

often in hand-to-_____ combat.
_{PART OF THE BODY}

2) The pistol. Since a pistol could only fire a single _____
_{NOUN}

without being reloaded, pirates often hid many loaded

_____ in the _____ they were wearing.
_{PLURAL NOUN} _{PLURAL NOUN}

The pistol was the female pirate's weapon of choice because it fit

_____ in the palm of her _____.
_{ADVERB} _{PART OF THE BODY}

3) The musket. Although it was very difficult to _____
_{VERB}

with gunpowder, a pirate with two good _____ and
_{PART OF THE BODY (PLURAL)}

a/an _____ hand could hit a bull's-_____
_{ADJECTIVE} _{NOUN}

nine times out of _____ with a musket.
_{NUMBER}

From PIRATES MAD LIBS® • Copyright © 2007 by Price Stern Sloan, a division of
Penguin Young Readers Group, 345 Hudson Street, New York, NY 10014.

MAD LIBS® is fun to play with friends, but you can also play it by yourself! To begin with, DO NOT look at the story on the page below. Fill in the blanks on this page with the words called for. Then, using the words you have selected, fill in the blank spaces in the story.

Now you've created your own hilarious MAD LIBS® game!

PIRATE MAKEOVER

ADJECTIVE _____

ADJECTIVE _____

NOUN _____

PERSON IN ROOM (MALE) _____

COLOR _____

PERSON IN ROOM (FEMALE) _____

NOUN _____

NOUN _____

PLURAL NOUN _____

PART OF THE BODY _____

NOUN _____

PART OF THE BODY _____

NOUN _____

VERB ENDING IN "ING" _____

NOUN _____

ADJECTIVE _____

PLURAL NOUN _____

ADJECTIVE _____

PLURAL NOUN _____

PLURAL NOUN _____

ADJECTIVE _____

PLURAL NOUN _____

MAD LIBS

PIRATE MAKEOVER

So you want to be a fierce and _____ pirate captain?
                                        ADJECTIVE

First you'll need a/an _____-sounding pirate name,
                              ADJECTIVE

such as _____ _____ or _____
              NOUN   PERSON IN ROOM (MALE)   COLOR

_____. You'll need a mascot, too, like a pet
PERSON IN ROOM (FEMALE)

_____, or even a/an _____ on your shoulder
        NOUN   NOUN

that says, "Aye, matey" and "Shiver me _____." Then
                                              PLURAL NOUN

you need to get a peg _____, put a sneer on your
                          PART OF THE BODY

_____, and wear a patch over your _____. And
        NOUN   PART OF THE BODY

every pirate captain needs a name for his or her ship. Your vessel

can be called *The Dreaded* _____, or *The* _____
                                  NOUN   VERB ENDING IN "ING"

_____. You can get all your _____
        NOUN   ADJECTIVE

friends together to raise the _____, swab the
                                    PLURAL NOUN

_____ _____, and hoist the skull-and-cross-
  ADJECTIVE   PLURAL NOUN

_____ flag. Now you're ready to sail the _____
  PLURAL NOUN   ADJECTIVE

seas looking for buried _____!
                              PLURAL NOUN

From PIRATES MAD LIBS® • Copyright © 2007 by Price Stern Sloan, a division of
Penguin Young Readers Group, 345 Hudson Street, New York, NY 10014.

MAD LIBS® is fun to play with friends, but you can also play it by yourself! To begin with, DO NOT look at the story on the page below. Fill in the blanks on this page with the words called for. Then, using the words you have selected, fill in the blank spaces in the story.

Now you've created your own hilarious MAD LIBS® game!

PIRATES AND SEA MONSTERS

ADJECTIVE _____

ADJECTIVE _____

NOUN _____

NOUN _____

NOUN _____

VERB _____

SAME VERB _____

PLURAL NOUN _____

PLURAL NOUN _____

PLURAL NOUN _____

NOUN _____

PERSON IN ROOM _____

NOUN _____

PLURAL NOUN _____

NOUN _____

VERB (PAST TENSE) _____

PART OF THE BODY _____

NOUN _____

PART OF THE BODY _____

NOUN _____

ADJECTIVE _____

MAD LIBS

PIRATES AND SEA MONSTERS

It was a/an _____ night, with fog so _____,
<u>ADJECTIVE</u>   <u>ADJECTIVE</u>

you could barely see your _____ in front of your
                                     <u>NOUN</u>

_____. The only sound was the groan of the tired
<u>NOUN</u>

_____ and the soft wind, which seemed to whisper,
<u>NOUN</u>

" _____ … _____ …" Suddenly, _____
   <u>VERB</u>   <u>SAME VERB</u>   <u>PLURAL NOUN</u>

shot out of the ocean like _____ on the Fourth
                         <u>PLURAL NOUN</u>

of July. *Bang! Pow!* They grabbed for _____ to
                                 <u>PLURAL NOUN</u>

bring down to the bottom of the sea—to Davy Jones's locker.

The dreaded _____ monster, _____, was
              <u>NOUN</u>   <u>PERSON IN ROOM</u>

as big as a giant _____ and it smelled like rotting
                   <u>NOUN</u>

_____. I hid inside a/an _____
<u>PLURAL NOUN</u>   <u>NOUN</u>

and _____ as the monster sucked the _____
    <u>VERB (PAST TENSE)</u>   <u>PART OF THE BODY</u>

right off one of my shipmates! I was scared out of my

_____, and my _____ almost stopped
      <u>NOUN</u>   <u>PART OF THE BODY</u>

beating! But, lucky for you, I escaped with my _____
                                      <u>NOUN</u>

and lived to tell the _____ tale!
                      <u>ADJECTIVE</u>

From PIRATES MAD LIBS® • Copyright © 2007 by Price Stern Sloan, a division of
Penguin Young Readers Group, 345 Hudson Street, New York, NY 10014.

MAD LIBS® is fun to play with friends, but you can also play it by yourself! To begin with, DO NOT look at the story on the page below. Fill in the blanks on this page with the words called for. Then, using the words you have selected, fill in the blank spaces in the story.

Now you've created your own hilarious MAD LIBS® game!

LOOKING FOR BURIED TREASURE

ADJECTIVE _____

PLURAL NOUN _____

ADJECTIVE _____

PLURAL NOUN _____

PLURAL NOUN _____

PLURAL NOUN _____

ADVERB _____

PLURAL NOUN _____

VERB _____

NOUN _____

ADJECTIVE _____

PLURAL NOUN _____

SILLY WORD _____

ADJECTIVE _____

NOUN _____

PLURAL NOUN _____

ADJECTIVE _____

NOUN _____

VERB _____

SAME VERB _____

MAD LIBS

LOOKING FOR BURIED TREASURE

Are ye looking to get _____ quick? If so, then ye must
ADJECTIVE

start searching for buried _____. It's a/an _____
PLURAL NOUN   ADJECTIVE

job, but ye might strike it rich and become a multimillionaire. I've

heard stories of pirates who found chests full of gold _____
PLURAL NOUN

and sparkling _____, and went on to build luxurious
PLURAL NOUN

_____ and live _____ ever after. But before ye
PLURAL NOUN   ADVERB

can find buried _____, ye'll need a map that shows
PLURAL NOUN

ye where to _____. Once ye've found the X that marks
VERB

the _____, start diggin'. It's best to use a/an _____
NOUN   ADJECTIVE

shovel, but if ye don't have one, yer bare _____ will
PLURAL NOUN

do. When ye hear _____, ye can stop diggin'. Pull out
SILLY WORD

the chest and look inside. There might be enough treasure inside to

make ye _____. But if ye've pulled out a/an _____
ADJECTIVE   NOUN

filled with sand and _____, don't feel too _____.
PLURAL NOUN   ADJECTIVE

It's not the end of the _____, matey. Ye know what they say:
NOUN

If at first ye don't succeed, _____, _____ again.
VERB   SAME VERB

From PIRATES MAD LIBS® • Copyright © 2007 by Price Stern Sloan, a division of
Penguin Young Readers Group, 345 Hudson Street, New York, NY 10014.

MAD LIBS® is fun to play with friends, but you can also play it by yourself! To begin with, DO NOT look at the story on the page below. Fill in the blanks on this page with the words called for. Then, using the words you have selected, fill in the blank spaces in the story.

Now you've created your own hilarious MAD LIBS® game!

A HISTORY OF PIRATE LADS

COLOR _____

ADJECTIVE _____

NOUN _____

NOUN _____

PLURAL NOUN _____

PLURAL NOUN _____

VERB _____

NOUN _____

PERSON IN ROOM (FEMALE) _____

NOUN _____

NOUN _____

PLURAL NOUN _____

NOUN _____

NOUN _____

NOUN _____

NOUN _____

PLURAL NOUN _____

ADJECTIVE _____

MAD LIBS

A HISTORY OF PIRATE LADS

Pretending to be a pirate is fun, but did you know that there were

real pirates who sailed the ocean _____? Have you heard of
                                   COLOR

Edward "Blackbeard" Teach? He was a/an _____ pirate with
                                          ADJECTIVE

a long black _____ that covered most of his _____.
              NOUN   NOUN

He would weave _____ into it and set them on fire to
                 PLURAL NOUN

strike fear in his enemies' _____. Another pirate, Francis
                              PLURAL NOUN

Drake, taught himself to _____. He learned every reef and
                           VERB

_____ in the Caribbean, and Queen _____
   NOUN   PERSON IN ROOM (FEMALE)

made him a/an _____ of the royal _____. She
                 NOUN   NOUN

even knighted him for his bravery and remarkable _____!
                                                    PLURAL NOUN

Captain Henry Morgan has a similar _____. He became a
                                      NOUN

commander of the English _____! Then there was William
                            NOUN

Kidd, whose pirate _____ was called *The Adventure*
                      NOUN

_____. At first, Kidd was reluctant to become a pirate and
   NOUN

start pillaging and plundering _____, but he ended up
                                 PLURAL NOUN

becoming a very successful, if _____, pirate.
                                 ADJECTIVE

From PIRATES MAD LIBS® • Copyright © 2007 by Price Stern Sloan, a division of
Penguin Young Readers Group, 345 Hudson Street, New York, NY 10014.

MAD LIBS® is fun to play with friends, but you can also play it by yourself! To begin with, DO NOT look at the story on the page below. Fill in the blanks on this page with the words called for. Then, using the words you have selected, fill in the blank spaces in the story.

Now you've created your own hilarious MAD LIBS® game!

A HISTORY OF PIRATE LADIES

VERB (PAST TENSE) _____

ADJECTIVE _____

VERB (PAST TENSE) _____

VERB _____

ADJECTIVE _____

PLURAL NOUN _____

ADJECTIVE _____

NOUN _____

ADJECTIVE _____

ADVERB _____

NOUN _____

VERB (PAST TENSE) _____

NOUN _____

PLURAL NOUN _____

PLURAL NOUN _____

NOUN _____

ADJECTIVE _____

A PLACE _____

PLURAL NOUN _____

MAD LIBS®

A HISTORY OF PIRATE LADIES

Now that you know about the male pirates who ______________ on
VERB (PAST TENSE)
the seven seas, you should learn a little about the ______________
ADJECTIVE
ladies who also ______________ and plundered. Generally, women
VERB (PAST TENSE)
weren't allowed to ______________ on pirate ships, but that
VERB
didn't stop them. They found ways to fool those ______________
ADJECTIVE
______________! First there was Anne Bonny, a/an ______________
PLURAL NOUN / ADJECTIVE
young ______________ of ______________ strength who had
NOUN / ADJECTIVE
a reputation for being ______________ handy with a/an
ADVERB
______________. Then there was Mary Read, who ______________
NOUN / VERB (PAST TENSE)
with Anne on the same ______________! Both of these female
NOUN
______________ dressed like ______________ to disguise themselves
PLURAL NOUN / PLURAL NOUN
aboard the ______________, *The Revenge*. Then there was Grace
NOUN
O'Malley—who wasn't just a pirate captain, but a/an ______________
ADJECTIVE
chieftain in (the) ______________, too! So you see, anything that
A PLACE
______________ could do, these women could do better!
PLURAL NOUN

From PIRATES MAD LIBS® • Copyright © 2007 by Price Stern Sloan, a division of
Penguin Young Readers Group, 345 Hudson Street, New York, NY 10014.

MAD LIBS® is fun to play with friends, but you can also play it by yourself! To begin with, DO NOT look at the story on the page below. Fill in the blanks on this page with the words called for. Then, using the words you have selected, fill in the blank spaces in the story.

Now you've created your own hilarious MAD LIBS® game!

PIRATE LIMERICKS

ADJECTIVE _____

PLURAL NOUN _____

PART OF THE BODY _____

ADJECTIVE _____

ADJECTIVE _____

ADJECTIVE _____

ADJECTIVE _____

NOUN _____

NOUN _____

VERB _____

VERB (PAST TENSE) _____

MAD LIBS
PIRATE LIMERICKS

Pirates love to sing _____ _____
                          ADJECTIVE   PLURAL NOUN

called limericks. Here are two favorites, usually on the tip of every

pirate's _____:
         PART OF THE BODY

A pretty, _____ pirate named Alice
              ADJECTIVE

Broke into the king's _____ palace.
                           ADJECTIVE

She caused a/an _____ scene,
                      ADJECTIVE

But she soon became queen—

That pretty, _____ pirate of malice.
                  ADJECTIVE

There once was a/an _____ named Billy.
                          NOUN

His _____-mates considered him quite silly.
         NOUN

He'd _____ up the mast
          VERB

While shouting, "Avast!"

As the ship _____ to Philly.
                VERB (PAST TENSE)

From PIRATES MAD LIBS® • Copyright © 2007 by Price Stern Sloan, a division of
Penguin Young Readers Group, 345 Hudson Street, New York, NY 10014.

MAD LIBS® is fun to play with friends, but you can also play it by yourself! To begin with, DO NOT look at the story on the page below. Fill in the blanks on this page with the words called for. Then, using the words you have selected, fill in the blank spaces in the story.

Now you've created your own hilarious MAD LIBS® game!

JOB OPPORTUNITY

VERB ENDING IN "ING" _____

NOUN _____

PERSON IN ROOM _____

ADJECTIVE _____

PLURAL NOUN _____

PLURAL NOUN _____

PLURAL NOUN _____

PLURAL NOUN _____

ADJECTIVE _____

PLURAL NOUN _____

ADJECTIVE _____

ADJECTIVE _____

NOUN _____

NOUN _____

NOUN _____

VERB _____

MAD LIBS

JOB OPPORTUNITY

ATTENTION!

The ship *The* _____ _____, commanded
VERB ENDING IN "ING"   NOUN

by Captain _____, offers a truly _____
PERSON IN ROOM   ADJECTIVE

opportunity to gain riches and everlasting _____ for
PLURAL NOUN

the following:

• Ten able-bodied _____. Needed for hoisting and trimming
PLURAL NOUN

the ship's _____, loading and firing _____, and
PLURAL NOUN   PLURAL NOUN

when necessary, swabbing the _____ _____.
ADJECTIVE   PLURAL NOUN

• Two lookouts. Must be blessed with _____ eyesight
ADJECTIVE

and _____ voices and be small enough to fit in a
ADJECTIVE

crow's _____.
NOUN

• One cabin _____. To be at the captain's beck and
NOUN

call morning, noon, and _____. Must be able to read
NOUN

and _____.
VERB

From PIRATES MAD LIBS® • Copyright © 2007 by Price Stern Sloan, a division of
Penguin Young Readers Group, 345 Hudson Street, New York, NY 10014.

MAD LIBS® is fun to play with friends, but you can also play it by yourself! To begin with, DO NOT look at the story on the page below. Fill in the blanks on this page with the words called for. Then, using the words you have selected, fill in the blank spaces in the story.

Now you've created your own hilarious MAD LIBS® game!

MORE THAN YOU NEED TO KNOW ABOUT PIRATES

ADJECTIVE _____

PLURAL NOUN _____

PLURAL NOUN _____

ADJECTIVE _____

PLURAL NOUN _____

NUMBER _____

PLURAL NOUN _____

ADJECTIVE _____

VERB _____

NOUN _____

PLURAL NOUN _____

PLURAL NOUN _____

PLURAL NOUN _____

NOUN _____

ADJECTIVE _____

ADVERB _____

PLURAL NOUN _____

PART OF THE BODY (PLURAL) _____

NOUN _____

MAD LIBS

MORE THAN YOU NEED TO KNOW ABOUT PIRATES

Pirates were known by many different _____
ADJECTIVE

names. They were called buccaneers, freebooters, corsairs,

and _____. A high percentage of pirates wore
PLURAL NOUN

beards and _____ to cover the _____
PLURAL NOUN   ADJECTIVE

scars on their faces. The average buccaneer was five feet, seven

_____ tall and weighed _____ _____.
PLURAL NOUN   NUMBER   PLURAL NOUN

Most freebooters were without any _____
ADJECTIVE

education. They could not _____ or even write their
VERB

own _____. Although pirates are portrayed in classic
NOUN

novels and motion _____ as romantic _____,
PLURAL NOUN   PLURAL NOUN

in truth, they were feisty _____ with a short
PLURAL NOUN

_____ and _____ tempers. They _____
NOUN   ADJECTIVE   ADVERB

believed that actions speak louder than _____ and,
PLURAL NOUN

armed to the _____, they would fight at the drop
PART OF THE BODY (PLURAL)

of a/an _____.
NOUN

From PIRATES MAD LIBS® • Copyright © 2007 by Price Stern Sloan, a division of
Penguin Young Readers Group, 345 Hudson Street, New York, NY 10014.

MAD LIBS® is fun to play with friends, but you can also play it by yourself! To begin with, DO NOT look at the story on the page below. Fill in the blanks on this page with the words called for. Then, using the words you have selected, fill in the blank spaces in the story.

Now you've created your own hilarious MAD LIBS® game!

PIRATE PETS

ADJECTIVE _____

NOUN _____

PART OF THE BODY _____

NOUN _____

PART OF THE BODY _____

NOUN _____

SILLY WORD _____

SILLY WORD _____

VERB _____

PLURAL NOUN _____

A PLACE _____

PLURAL NOUN _____

ADJECTIVE _____

PLURAL NOUN _____

MAD LIBS

PIRATE PETS

When I think of a pirate, I picture a/an _____ _____
ADJECTIVE   NOUN

with a peg _____, a/an _____ over his or her
PART OF THE BODY   NOUN

eye, and a parrot perched atop his or her _____. And
PART OF THE BODY

whenever that parrot sees a/an _____ in the distance,
NOUN

it goes, "_____, _____," and the crew
SILLY WORD   SILLY WORD

gets ready to _____. But that's not accurate—pirates
VERB

may have brought parrots aboard their _____, but
PLURAL NOUN

not as pets. Instead, they would bring them back to (the)

_____. Parrots were considered highly exotic, and were
A PLACE

worth a lot of _____. The only pets that pirates
PLURAL NOUN

probably had on board were _____ cats. And what did
ADJECTIVE

the cats do? That's right—they kept the _____ away!
PLURAL NOUN

Here, kitty, kitty!

From PIRATES MAD LIBS® • Copyright © 2007 by Price Stern Sloan, a division of
Penguin Young Readers Group, 345 Hudson Street, New York, NY 10014.

MAD LIBS® is fun to play with friends, but you can also play it by yourself! To begin with, DO NOT look at the story on the page below. Fill in the blanks on this page with the words called for. Then, using the words you have selected, fill in the blank spaces in the story.

Now you've created your own hilarious MAD LIBS® game!

MISSING TREASURE

NOUN _____

PERSON IN ROOM _____

NOUN _____

A PLACE _____

VERB (PAST TENSE) _____

SAME PERSON IN ROOM _____

SAME PERSON IN ROOM _____

NOUN _____

PLURAL NOUN _____

CELEBRITY _____

ADJECTIVE _____

SAME PERSON IN ROOM _____

TYPE OF LIQUID _____

SAME PERSON IN ROOM _____

COLOR _____

ADJECTIVE _____

VERB _____

MAD LIBS

MISSING TREASURE

Pirate Captain _____-face _____
                    NOUN   PERSON IN ROOM

stormed out of his/her cabin. "Argh!" he/she cried. "Who stole me

candy _____? I was savin' it for a special occasion.
            NOUN

It's the tastiest candy this side of (the) _____!" The
                                                  A PLACE

crew members _____ in their boots. No one wanted
                    VERB (PAST TENSE)

to make Captain _____ angry. You never knew what
                    SAME PERSON IN ROOM

he'd/she'd do. "I'll only be askin' one more time, mateys," Captain

_____ bellowed. "Who stole me candy? If ye don't
SAME PERSON IN ROOM

confess, every last one of ye will walk the _____ and
                                                        NOUN

swim with the _____." Just then, _____,
                    PLURAL NOUN   CELEBRITY

the crew's _____ monkey, climbed onto Captain
                    ADJECTIVE

_____'s shoulder. Its face was covered in
SAME PERSON IN ROOM

_____. Captain _____'s face became
    TYPE OF LIQUID   SAME PERSON IN ROOM

_____ with rage. "Ye _____ monkey!"
    COLOR   ADJECTIVE

he/she shouted. "Ye stole me candy! I hope ye can _____,
                                                              VERB

because yer going overboard!"

From PIRATES MAD LIBS® • Copyright © 2007 by Price Stern Sloan, a division of
Penguin Young Readers Group, 345 Hudson Street, New York, NY 10014.

This book is published by

PSS!

PRICE STERN SLOAN

whose other splendid titles include such literary classics as

The Original #1 Mad Libs®
Son of Mad Libs®
Sooper Dooper Mad Libs®
Monster Mad Libs®
Goofy Mad Libs®
Off-the-Wall Mad Libs®
Vacation Fun Mad Libs®
Camp Daze Mad Libs®
Christmas Fun Mad Libs®
Dinosaur Mad Libs®
Mad Libs® 40th Anniversary Deluxe Edition
Mad Mad Mad Mad Mad Libs®
Mad Libs® On the Road
The Apprentice™ Mad Libs®
The Powerpuff Girls™ Mad Libs®
Scooby-Doo!™ Mad Libs®
Flushed Away™ Mad Libs®
Happy Feet™ Mad Libs®
Madagascar™ Mad Libs®
Over the Hedge™ Mad Libs®
Operation™ Mad Libs®
SpongeBob SquarePants™ Mad Libs®
Fear Factor™ Mad Libs®
Fear Factor™ Mad Libs®: Ultimate Gross Out!
Survivor™ Mad Libs®
Guinness World Records™ Mad Libs®
Betty and Veronica® Mad Libs®
Napoleon Dynamite™ Mad Libs®
Nancy Drew® Mad Libs®
The Mad Libs® Worst-Case Scenario™ Survival Handbook
The Mad Libs® Worst-Case Scenario™ Survival Handbook 2

and many, many more!
Mad Libs® are available wherever books are sold.